D1071059

Kobe Bryant

by A. R. Schaefer

Reading Consultant:
Dr. Robert Miller
Professor of Special Education
Minnesota State University, Mankato

CAPSTONE
HIGH-INTEREST
BOOKS

an imprint of Capstone Press
Mankato, Minnesota

Capstone High-Interest Books are published by Capstone Press
151 Good Counsel Drive, P.O. Box 669, Mankato, Minnesota 56002
http://www.capstone-press.com

Library of Congress Cataloging-in-Publication Data
Schaefer, Adam.
  Kobe Bryant/by A. R. Schaefer
  p. cm.—(Sports heroes)
  Includes bibliographical references (p. 45) and index.
  Summary: Traces the life and basketball career of All-Star guard, Kobe Bryant.
  ISBN 0-7368-1052-8
  1. Bryant, Kobe, 1978—Juvenile literature. 2. Basketball players—United
States—Biography—Juvenile literature. [1. Bryant, Kobe, 1978– 2. Basketball
players. 3. African Americans—Biography.] I. Title. II. Sports heroes (Mankato,
Minn.)
GV884.B794 S34 2002
796.323'092—dc21   2001003633

Editorial Credits

Matt Doeden, editor; Timothy Halldin, cover and interior designer; Katy Kudela,
  photo researcher

Photo Credits

ALLSPORT PHOTOGRAPHY/Jed Jacobsohn, 4, 7, 9, 21; Doug Pensinger, 15; Vince
  Bucci, 16; Lou Capozzola NBA, 18; Todd Warshaw, 22; Donald Miralle, 24;
  Harry How, 27; Tom Hauck, 28, 31; Steve Grayson, 32; Ezra O. Shaw, 36, 38
Reuters/Mike Blake/Archive Photos, 41
SportsChrome-USA/Michael Zito, 10, 42; Brian Spurlock, cover, 12, 34

1 2 3 4 5 6 07 06 05 04 03 02

Table of Contents

CHAPTER 1

Overtime Thriller

On June 14, 2000, the Los Angeles Lakers were playing the Indiana Pacers in the National Basketball Association (NBA) Finals in Indianapolis, Indiana. It was the fourth game of the series. The Lakers had won two of the first three games.

The teams were tied at the end of the fourth quarter. They went into a 5-minute overtime. In the overtime period, Laker center Shaquille O'Neal fouled out of the game. Most people considered O'Neal the NBA's best player. Many fans believed the Pacers would win the game with O'Neal on the bench.

Kobe Bryant and the Lakers faced the Pacers in the 2000 NBA Finals.

Laker guard Kobe Bryant had suffered an ankle injury earlier in the series. His ankle still was not as strong as it normally was. But Kobe knew his teammates needed him to play his best. The Lakers did not want to let the Pacers tie the series.

The Pacers scored a basket after O'Neal left the game. More than 18,000 fans stood and cheered loudly. But Kobe quickly ran down the floor and made a long jump shot. The shot gave the Lakers a three-point lead.

The Pacers continued to make baskets. But Kobe did not let his teammates give up. With only seconds left, the game was tied. Laker guard Brian Shaw missed a jump shot. But Kobe jumped high to grab the ball and put it through the basket. Kobe's basket gave the Lakers a 120-118 victory.

Kobe scored 28 points in the game. Eight of his points came in overtime. The Lakers later went on to win the NBA championship.

Kobe scored eight points in overtime to lead the Lakers to victory in the fourth game.

About Kobe Bryant

Kobe Bryant is the starting shooting guard for the Los Angeles Lakers. He has played for the Lakers since 1996. He helped the Lakers win the NBA championship in 2000 and 2001.

Kobe is one of the biggest stars in the NBA. Some people compare him to NBA great Michael Jordan. Like Jordan, Kobe plays well on both offense and defense. He is a good shooter and also can drive to the basket. Jordan and Kobe are nearly the same size. Kobe stands 6 feet, 7 inches (201 centimeters) tall. He is 1 inch (2.5 centimeters) taller than Jordan. Some people think Kobe looks and speaks like Jordan.

Kobe also is successful off the court. He earns millions of dollars each year by endorsing products such as Adidas shoes and Sprite. He appears in advertisements to help these companies sell their products.

Kobe Bryant

NBA Per-Game Statistics

Year	Team	Games	Points	Rebounds	Steals	Assists
96–97	LAL	71	7.6	1.9	0.69	1.3
97–98	LAL	79	15.4	3.1	0.94	2.5
98–99	LAL	50	19.9	5.3	1.44	3.8
99–00	LAL	66	22.5	6.3	1.61	4.9
00–01	LAL	68	28.5	5.9	1.68	5.0
Career		334	18.5	4.4	1.24	3.4

CHAPTER 2

The Early Years

Kobe was born August 23, 1978, in Philadelphia, Pennsylvania. He is the youngest child of Pamela and Joe Bryant. Kobe's parents named him for a kind of steak served at a restaurant. Kobe's parents ate at this restaurant before Kobe was born. Kobe has two older sisters named Sharia and Shaya.

Joe was a professional basketball player. His nickname as a basketball player was "Jelly Bean." Joe played in the NBA during the late 1970s and early 1980s.

Life in Italy
Joe got a job playing basketball in Italy after he retired from the NBA. The Bryant family moved

Kobe was born August 23, 1978.

Kobe dreamed of playing in the NBA someday.

to Rieti, Italy. Kobe and his family lived in Italy for eight years. They moved around the country several times when Joe changed teams. Kobe learned to speak Italian. He also became interested in basketball.

Some of Kobe's family members in the United States sent him videotapes of NBA games. Kobe enjoyed watching the NBA players. He asked his family members for more tapes.

> After school, I would be on the basketball court, working on my moves, and then kids would start showing up with their soccer ball. It was either go home or be the goalkeeper.
> —Kobe Bryant, *Sports Illustrated*, 4/27/98

Joe and Kobe watched the tapes together. They talked about the players' moves and what they might have been thinking. Kobe learned about the game from watching these tapes and talking with his father.

After school, Kobe sometimes went to Joe's basketball practices. He watched the players go through drills. He practiced his shooting while the team worked out on another court. Kobe also attended Joe's games. He sometimes went onto the court during halftime to shoot baskets. The crowds cheered for him as he shot.

Kobe watched Joe on TV when he could not attend games. He sometimes set up a small hoop in front of the TV. Kobe copied his father's moves. He shot when Joe shot. He took a drink when Joe took a drink. Kobe imagined himself playing on TV someday.

Returning to the United States

When Kobe was 13, his family moved back to the Philadelphia area. Kobe joined a summer basketball league near his home. He later made the varsity team at Lower Merion High School in Ardmore, Pennsylvania.

Kobe's skills continued to improve. He was an instant success on his high school team. He was named a starter when he was in ninth grade. When Kobe was 16, he beat Joe in a game of one-on-one.

Kobe quickly became the star of Lower Merion's team. He was an excellent scorer. He scored 50 points during one game. He could rebound and pass well. He also was one of the best defenders among all U.S. high school players.

Kobe went to a basketball camp during the summer after 11th grade. At the camp, he was named Most Valuable Player. Many college coaches were at the camp. They were impressed by Kobe's skills. Most of them wanted Kobe to play for their teams.

Kobe's First Championship

Kobe led Lower Merion's team to the playoffs during his last high school season. In one

Kobe was named to the McDonald's All-American Team after his final high school season.

playoff game, he scored 34 points and grabbed 15 rebounds. He also had six assists and blocked nine shots.

Lower Merion went on to win the 1996 Pennsylvania Class AAAA state championship. The team finished the season 31-3. Kobe averaged 30.8 points, 12 rebounds, 6.5 assists, four steals, and almost four blocked shots per game during the season.

A HERO'S HERO

Magic Johnson

Kobe watched many NBA basketball players as he grew up. One of his favorite players was Laker point guard Ervin "Magic" Johnson.

Johnson had a long and successful basketball career. In 1979, he led the Michigan State Spartans to the NCAA basketball championship. The Lakers drafted Johnson with their first pick later that year.

Johnson led the Lakers to five NBA championships. He won the NBA's Most Valuable Player award twice. He helped lead Team USA to a gold medal in the 1992 Olympics. The NBA also named Johnson one of the 50 greatest players in the history of the league.

Kobe won many awards at the end of the season. He was named to the McDonald's All-American Team. The best high school players in the country are named to this team. *USA Today* newspaper and *Parade Magazine* named Kobe "National High School Player of the Year." Most experts agreed that Kobe was the best high school basketball player in the United States.

Big Decision

Kobe thought about going to college to play basketball. All of the top college basketball programs recruited him. These schools included Michigan, Duke, and North Carolina.

Kobe had a different plan. In 1995, Kevin Garnett skipped college and went directly to the NBA. The Minnesota Timberwolves selected Garnett with the fifth pick in the 1995 NBA Draft. Garnett then proved he could play in the NBA at a young age.

Kobe had always dreamed of playing in the NBA. He wanted to do the same thing Garnett had done. On April 29, 1996, Kobe announced that he wanted to enter the 1996 NBA Draft.

CHAPTER 3

A Big Jump

The Lakers were one of the teams that badly wanted to draft Kobe. But the Lakers had the 24th pick. Laker officials did not believe Kobe would still be available for their turn to pick. The Lakers talked to other teams about trading for Kobe.

The Charlotte Hornets selected Kobe with the 13th pick. But the Hornets did not pick Kobe for themselves. Instead, they traded him to the Lakers for center Vlade Divac. Kobe then signed a three-year contract to play for the Lakers. The contract paid Kobe $3.5 million.

NBA commissioner David Stern congratulated Kobe after the Hornets selected him in the draft.

NBA Beginnings

Kobe practiced all summer and entered training camp that fall. He worked hard to learn the Lakers' plays. Kobe's first game was against the Timberwolves on November 3, 1996. He was the youngest player to ever appear in an NBA game. He was 18 years, two months, and 11 days old.

Kobe did not play much in his first game. He missed the only shot he took. But he continued to work on his skills. He wanted to learn from his teammates and from other NBA players.

Kobe grew more confident as the season continued. He started a game for the first time on January 28, 1997. He was the youngest player ever to start in an NBA game.

One of the highlights of Kobe's rookie season occurred during the All-Star break. The NBA hosted a rookie game the day before the All-Star Game. The league's best first-year players competed in this game. Kobe was the star of the game. He scored 31 points. Kobe

Kobe averaged 7.6 points per game during the 1996–97 season.

also won the slam dunk competition. His best dunk earned 49 out of 50 possible points. People quickly noticed Kobe's skills.

Kobe played better in the second half of the 1996–97 season. He scored 24 points against the Golden State Warriors on April 8, 1997. He missed only two shots in the game.

Kobe and the Lakers reached the playoffs. Kobe scored 22 points in a first-round game

Kobe started in only one game during the 1997–98 season.

against the Portland Trailblazers. He scored 19 points in a second-round game against the Utah Jazz. But the Jazz won the series and knocked the Lakers out of the playoffs.

Becoming a Star

Kobe played more during the 1997–98 season. But he started only one game. He averaged 15.4 points per game during the regular season.

On December 17, 1997, the Lakers played the Chicago Bulls at the United Center in Chicago. Most people believed that the Bulls were the best team in the NBA. Michael Jordan played for the Bulls. Kobe was excited to play against Jordan. Kobe scored 33 points in the game. It was the best game he had ever played. But Jordan scored 36 points. The Bulls won the game 104-83.

NBA fans became excited about Kobe's skills. The fans voted Kobe as a Western Conference starter in the All-Star Game. No reserve player had ever been named an All-Star starter before.

Kobe was the youngest player ever to compete in an All-Star Game. Kobe scored 18 points in the game. He also grabbed six rebounds. But the Eastern Conference beat the Western Conference 132-120.

Later that season, the Lakers beat Portland in the first round of the playoffs. In the second round, they beat the Seattle Supersonics. But they lost to the Jazz in the next round.

CHAPTER 4

NBA Starter

The 1998–99 season was delayed because of a lockout. The owners and players could not agree on how much money players should be allowed to earn. The season did not begin until early 1999.

A Disappointing Season

The Lakers did not plan to make Kobe a starter in 1999. But starter Rick Fox was injured at the start of the season. Kobe started instead. He scored 25 points and had 10 rebounds in his first game.

Kobe continued to play well as a starter. The Lakers decided to keep him in the

Kobe became a regular starter for the Lakers in 1999.

starting lineup. Kobe then started all 50 regular-season games for the Lakers. He averaged nearly 20 points per game.

The Lakers finished the shortened season with a record of 31-19. They again made the playoffs. Many people believed that the Lakers could win the championship.

The Lakers played the Houston Rockets in the first round of the playoffs. Kobe scored 24 points in the fourth game. His effort helped the Lakers advance to the second round.

In the second round, the Lakers played the San Antonio Spurs. But the Spurs were too strong for the Lakers. The Spurs won the first four games to sweep the Lakers. Once again, the Lakers' season was over.

A Great Season
The 1999–2000 season was a big one for Kobe and the Lakers. The Lakers were the best team in the NBA during the regular season. Their record was 67-15. Kobe averaged 22.5 points and 6.3 rebounds per game.

The Lakers lost to the Spurs in the second round of the 1999 playoffs.

Not everyone was happy with Kobe's performance. Some people said that Kobe was a selfish player. They complained that he did not pass often enough. They said that he took too many shots. But Kobe did not change the way he played. He remained confident in his ability.

The Lakers began the playoffs against the Sacramento Kings. The teams split the first four games of the series. Kobe scored 17 points in the fifth game to help the Lakers win the series.

The Lakers met the Phoenix Suns in the second round. They easily beat the Suns four games to one. The Lakers had finally advanced beyond the second round of the playoffs.

Next, the Lakers played Portland for the Western Conference championship. The winner would advance to the NBA Finals. The teams split the first six games. Game seven would determine the winner.

Kobe scored 25 points in the seventh game to help the Lakers defeat the Trailblazers.

The Lakers did not begin the game well. They trailed by 15 points early in the fourth quarter. The Trailblazers appeared set to go to the NBA Finals.

The Lakers were not ready to quit. They went on to outscore the Trailblazers 25-5 in the game's final minutes. Kobe made two free throws that put the Lakers ahead for good. He scored 25 points in the game. He also had 11 rebounds, seven assists, and four blocked shots.

NBA Finals

Kobe and the Lakers faced the Indiana Pacers in the NBA Finals. It was the first time since 1991 that the Lakers had made the NBA Finals. The first two games were in Los Angeles. Kobe scored only 14 points in the first game. But Shaquille O'Neal scored 43 points to lead the Lakers to victory.

Kobe sprained his ankle 9 minutes into the second game. The injury prevented him from

Kobe scored 26 points in the last game of the 2000 NBA Finals.

returning to the game. But O'Neal scored 40 points. The Lakers won the game.

The next three games took place in Indianapolis, Indiana. Kobe's ankle still hurt before the third game. He did not play. The Pacers won the game 100-91.

Kobe was able to play in the fourth game. He scored 28 points in this game. Eight of his points came in overtime. The Lakers won 120-118.

The Lakers played poorly in the fifth game. The Pacers won easily. But the Lakers led the series 3-2.

The series returned to Los Angeles for the sixth game. The Pacers played well. They led the Lakers 84-79 to begin the fourth quarter. But the Lakers came back late in the quarter. Kobe scored 26 points and had 10 rebounds as the Lakers won 116-111. The Lakers won the NBA championship for the first time since 1988.

Kobe held the championship trophy during a celebration after the NBA Finals.

CHAPTER 5

Kobe Bryant Today

Kobe continued his success in the 2000–01 season. He finished fourth in the NBA in scoring with a 28.5 points per game average. The Lakers won the Pacific Division with a 56-26 record.

Kobe also was successful during the playoffs. He averaged 25 points per game in the Lakers' first playoff series against the Trailblazers. The Lakers swept Portland in the series.

Kobe finished fourth in the league in scoring during the 2000-01 season. He averaged 28.5 points per game.

The Lakers faced the Kings in the second round. Once again, the Lakers dominated the series. They won the first four games to sweep the Kings. Kobe scored 48 points and had 16 rebounds in the final game. He averaged 35 points per game in the series.

The Lakers faced the Spurs in the Western Conference championship. Many NBA experts believed the two teams were evenly matched. But the Lakers again won the first four games. They swept the Spurs and advanced to the NBA Finals. Kobe scored 45 points in the first game. He averaged 33.3 points per game during the series.

Another Championship

The Lakers faced the Philadelphia 76ers in the NBA Finals. Few people expected the 76ers to win the series. The first two games were in Los Angeles. The 76ers won the first game 107-101. Kobe played poorly during this game. He made only seven of his 22 shots. He also turned over the ball six times.

Kobe returned to his hometown of Philadelphia for the 2001 NBA Finals.

> Winning a first championship is like a honeymoon. You just have to prove to everybody that we could do it. This time around, we went through so much adversity, so many ups and downs. It feels good to win it.
> —Kobe Bryant, ESPN.com, 6/15/01

Kobe and the Lakers did not lose their confidence after the loss. In the second game, Kobe scored 31 points to lead the Lakers to a 98-89 win. The series then moved to Philadelphia. Kobe was excited to play in his hometown. But many Philadelphia fans booed him when he stepped onto the court.

The Lakers won the next two games to take a 3-1 series lead. They then won the last game 108-96 to claim the championship. Kobe averaged 24.6 points per game in the series.

Kobe off the Court

Kobe remains close with his family. He married Vanessa Laine on April 18, 2001. The wedding took place just before the beginning of the 2001 playoffs.

Kobe understands that he has more money and success than most people have. He knows that many children grow up in difficult situations. In 1998, Kobe formed the Kobe Bryant Foundation to help these children.

Kobe and his teammates celebrated their second straight NBA championship after beating the 76ers.

Kobe's foundation gives money to groups in the Los Angeles area that help children. These groups include the Boys Clubs and Girls Clubs. Kobe hosts a bowling event every year to raise money for the foundation. Many celebrities attend the event and bowl to help Kobe raise money.

Kobe helps children in other ways. He spends some of his free time with children who need a positive role model. He sometimes speaks to groups of children about how to succeed in life. Kobe hopes that his influence on children will help them to lead better lives.

Kobe married Vanessa Laine April 18, 2001.

Career Highlights

1978—Kobe is born in Philadelphia, Pennsylvania, on August 23.

1992—Kobe starts for Lower Merion High School's varsity team as a ninth-grader.

1995—Kobe is named Most Valuable Player of the Adidas ABCD Summer Camp.

1996—Kobe leads Lower Merion to the Class AAAA state championship; he declares himself eligible for the NBA Draft and is drafted by the Charlotte Hornets; the Hornets trade him to the Los Angeles Lakers; Kobe plays his first NBA game on November 3.

1997—Kobe starts in his first NBA game on January 28; he wins the 1996-97 Slam Dunk championship; on December 17, he scores 33 points against the Bulls.

1998—Kobe becomes the youngest player to ever play in an NBA All-Star Game; he scores 18 points in the game.

1999—Kobe becomes a full-time starter; he averages nearly 20 points per game in the regular season.

2000—Kobe and the Lakers win the NBA championship by beating the Indiana Pacers.

2001—Kobe is fourth in the NBA in scoring with 28.5 points per game; the Lakers defeat the 76ers to claim their second straight NBA title.

Words to Know

contract (KON-trakt)—a legal agreement between a team and a player; contracts determine players' salaries.

endorse (en-DORSS)—to sponsor a product by appearing in advertisements

lockout (LOK-out)—a period of time in which owners prevent players from reporting to their teams; owners do not pay players during a lockout.

recruit (ri-KROOT)—to try to convince someone to join a group; college basketball coaches recruit high school players to play on their teams.

rookie (RUK-ee)—a first-year player

sprain (SPRAYN)—to injure a joint by twisting or tearing its muscles or ligaments

To Learn More

Coffey, Wayne R. *The Kobe Bryant Story.* Fast Breaks. New York: Scholastic Inc., 1999.

Kennedy, Nick. *Kobe Bryant: Star Guard.* Sports Reports. Berkeley Heights, N.J.: Enslow Publishers, 2002.

Savage, Jeff. *Kobe Bryant: Basketball Big Shot.* Minneapolis: LernerSports, 2001.

Stewart, Mark. *Kobe Bryant: Hard to the Hoop.* Basketball's New Wave. Brookfield, Conn.: Millbrook Press, 2000.

Useful Addresses

Kobe Bryant
c/o Los Angeles Lakers
Staples Center
1111 South Figueroa Street
Los Angeles, CA 90015

Naismith Memorial Basketball Hall of Fame
1150 West Columbus Avenue
Springfield, MA 01105

National Basketball Association
645 5th Avenue
New York, NY 10022

Internet Sites

CNNsi.com—Kobe Bryant
http://sportsillustrated.cnn.com/basketball/nba/
 players/3118

ESPN.com—Kobe Bryant
http://sports.espn.go.com/nba/players/
 profile?statsId=3118

NBA.com
http://nba.com

Official Site of the Los Angeles Lakers
http://www.nba.com/lakers

Index